THE PERSISTENT GARDENER
A TALE OF DREAMS AND REMEMBERING

Copyright © [Robin Whimsy], [2024]

All rights reserved.

THE PERSISTENT GARDENER

Sam woke up with a start, his heart pounding. The clock on his bedside table glowed 7:30 AM — his usual running time had slipped past him. He jumped out of bed, already feeling the weight of another forgotten promise hanging over him.

Today was supposed to be the day he would finally get his garden in shape, but now he was running late.

Quickly pulling on his sneakers, Sam dashed downstairs,

grabbing a piece of toast.

As he ate, he tried to shake off the anxious feeling that seeed to follow him every morning. "I can do this," he muttered to himself, trying to muster enthusiasm. "I'll get to the garden, then go for my run."

Sam's backyard was a chaotic mix of potential and neglect. The once-rich soil was now overgrown with weeds, and the seeds he had so carefully planted a few weeks ago were barely visible.

He had been so excited to start his garden — dreaming of colorful flowers and fresh vegetables. But now, as he looked at the sad, dry patches, Sam's excitement was overshadowed by frustration.

He hurried outside, his heart sinking as he saw the state of his garden. The marigolds, sunflowers, and tomato plants were struggling, their leaves wilted and brown.

He had forgotten to water them for days, and it showed. The garden, which had once seemed like a magical place full of promise, now looked like a collection of dying dreams.

Sam's hands shook slightly as he picked up the watering can. He poured water over the plants, trying to revive them, but it was clear that too much damage had been done. His shoulders slumped in defeat.

"Why can't I remember to do this?" he asked, more to himself than to anyone else. His frustration was palpable, and tears of helplessness started to form.

After a few minutes of watering, Sam glanced at his watch and realized he had missed his running time. He quickly switched gears, grabbing his running gear and heading out the door. As he jogged down the path, he tried to focus on his breathing, but his mind kept wandering.

He thought about the running schedule he had set up —
one he had been so excited about. Yet, here he was, missing
another run because he had forgotten again.

By the time he returned home, sweaty and defeated, Sam
felt like he was caught in a never-ending cycle of starting
strong and then falling short.

The garden wasn't the only thing that suffered; his
running was inconsistent, and even his reading goals were
slipping away.

He remembered starting a new book on productivity, but
the bookmark was lost, and the book itself lay forgotten
under his bed.

Feeling overwhelmed, Sam slumped into a chair at the kitchen table. He pulled out his goal notebook, a gift from his mom, which was meant to help him track his progress. The pages were filled with dreams and plans — gardening tips, running schedules, and reading lists. But as he flipped through the pages, he was struck by the sight of so many unfinished goals.

His mom walked in, noticing his distress. "Morning, Sam. How's everything going with your garden and running?" she asked gently.

Sam looked up, his face filled with frustration and a touch of shame. "I don't know, Mom. I keep forgetting things. I wanted to make my garden beautiful, run faster, and read more, but I keep messing up. It feels like I start with great ideas and then just…forget."

His mom sat down beside him, her eyes filled with understanding. "It sounds like you're really trying hard, Sam. Remember, it's okay to need some help with remembering. Maybe we can figure out a way to keep track of things better."

Sam nodded, feeling a bit of relief at her support but still overwhelmed by the enormity of his struggles. "I hope so. I just don't know how to make myself remember. It's like I'm stuck in this loop of forgetting and failing."

The weight of his challenges felt heavy, but Sam's mom placed a comforting hand on his shoulder. "Let's start by breaking things down into smaller steps. We can find ways to help you remember and stay on track. You're not alone in this."

Sam looked at his goal notebook again, his mind racing with the enormity of his dreams and the seemingly insurmountable obstacles ahead. He knew he needed to find a way to break free from the cycle of forgetting, but he didn't know where to start.

As he sat there, a mix of frustration and determination in his heart, Sam realized that this journey was not just about planting seeds and running laps. It was about learning to navigate the challenges of ADHD and discovering how to turn his dreams into reality, one step at a time.

The next morning, Sam's alarm clock rang earlier than usual. He groggily rolled out of bed, determined to get his day back on track. Today was the day he would start fresh. With renewed hope, Sam headed to his garden, hoping to see signs of improvement from his efforts yesterday.

As he stepped outside, the sunlight warmed his face, but Sam's mood quickly shifted. His garden still looked tired. The marigolds and sunflowers hadn't perked up much, and the tomato plants seemed to be struggling more than ever.

Sam sighed, feeling a wave of disappointment wash over him.

His mom joined him in the garden, noticing his downcast expression. "Morning, Sam. How are the plants doing today?"

Sam ran a hand through his hair, his frustration evident. "They're not doing well, Mom. I tried to water them yesterday, but it's like they're not getting any better. I keep forgetting to take care of them, and now I'm not sure if they'll ever recover."

His mom knelt beside him, gently touching a drooping sunflower. "Sometimes, plants need a bit of extra care to bounce back. It might take a little more time. Have you thought about setting up reminders for yourself?"

Sam nodded, looking thoughtful. "I've tried setting reminders before, but I keep forgetting to check them. It's like the reminders disappear from my mind."

His mom smiled gently. "Let's brainstorm some ideas together. Maybe we can use a visual cue or a routine to help you remember."

As they talked, Sam's dad came out with a cup of hot cocoa. "I heard you guys talking about the garden. I've been thinking about how we might help Sam keep track of his goals. What if we created a simple chart with checkboxes for each task? That way, Sam can see his progress and stay motivated."

Sam's eyes brightened at the idea. "That sounds like it might work. I could use something like that to keep track of watering the plants and other tasks."

His dad nodded. "We can make it colorful and place it somewhere you'll see it often, like on the kitchen fridge. Visual reminders can help a lot."

Sam felt a flicker of hope. Maybe this was the solution he needed. "Okay, let's give it a try."

Later that day, Sam and his parents sat down to create the chart. They used bright markers and stickers to make it fun. Sam added columns for watering the garden, running practice, and reading time. They hung it on the fridge, right at eye level.

As Sam worked on the chart, he shared his worries with his parents. "I really want to do well with my goals. I keep starting things with so much excitement, but then I forget and get frustrated."

His mom put a comforting hand on his shoulder. "It's okay to have setbacks, Sam. What's important is that you're trying to find solutions and asking for help. That's a big part of achieving your goals."

Sam nodded, feeling reassured. "I know. I just need to remember to stick with it, even when it's hard."

With the new chart in place, Sam felt a sense of accomplishment. It was a small step, but it felt like a big one towards getting back on track. He decided to take a few moments to review his running schedule and make a plan for his reading as well.

That evening, Sam sat down with his book, determined to make progress. As he read, he set a timer on his phone to remind him when it was time to put the book down and move on to his next task. He hoped that these small changes would help him keep his goals in sight.

The days that followed were a mix of successes and challenges. Sam tried his best to stick to his chart, but there were moments when he still forgot. Each time, though, he would review his chart and try to refocus. He started to see that progress didn't come all at once, but with consistent effort and adjustments.

One afternoon, while watering the garden, Sam noticed a tiny sprout pushing through the soil. It wasn't much, but it was a sign of hope. He felt a surge of encouragement, knowing that even with his struggles, he was making a difference.

Sam's mom came out to join him, smiling at the sight of the sprout. "Look at that, Sam! Your hard work is starting to pay off."

Sam beamed with pride. "It's not much, but it's a start. I'm going to keep working at it and do my best to remember my tasks."

His mom gave him a supportive hug. "That's the spirit. Remember, every small step counts. Keep believing in yourself and your goals."

Sam watched as the sprout swayed gently in the breeze,

feeling a renewed sense of determination. He knew that the journey ahead would be filled with ups and downs, but with the support of his family and his new strategies, he felt more equipped to face the challenges.

The next morning, Sam was determined to stick to his new routine. After a quick breakfast, he grabbed his running shoes and headed outside. The sky was clear, and the crisp morning air felt refreshing. Today was his chance to start making consistent progress.

As he laced up his shoes, Sam's friend, Jake, came jogging up the driveway. Jake was always full of energy and had a knack for remembering his schedules and goals.

"Hey, Sam! Ready for our run?" Jake called out, a friendly grin on his face.

Sam forced a smile. "Yeah, I'm ready. I've been trying to stick to a routine, but it's been tough."

Jake looked concerned. "What do you mean? You're doing great! What's been going on?"

Sam sighed, stretching before starting his run. "I keep forgetting my goals. I wanted to run every morning, work on my garden, and read more, but I keep losing track. It's like I start with so much motivation, and then… poof, it's gone."

Jake nodded sympathetically. "I get it. I've heard that managing goals can be tough when you're dealing with ADHD. Maybe we can come up with some strategies together."

Sam's eyes lit up. "That would be awesome. I could really use some help."

As they jogged through the park, Jake shared some ideas. "Have you tried using apps or alarms on your phone to remind you? I've heard they can be really helpful for staying on track."

Sam shook his head. "I've tried setting reminders, but I often forget to check them. It's like they're not even there."

Jake thought for a moment. "What about using a visual planner? You can keep it with you, so you always see it. Plus, writing things down can help reinforce your memory."

Sam looked thoughtful. "That sounds like it might work. I could use a planner to keep track of everything and keep it somewhere visible."

Jake smiled. "Great! And if you ever need a running buddy or someone to check in with, I'm here for you. We can motivate each other."

Sam felt a wave of relief. "Thanks, Jake. I really appreciate your support. It makes a big difference."

After their run, Sam and Jake headed to the local library to meet up with Sam's ADHD coach, Ms. Lee. Ms. Lee was known for her patience and expertise in helping kids with ADHD manage their goals.

When they arrived, Ms. Lee greeted them warmly. "Good morning, Sam. Jake. Ready to work on some new strategies today?"

Sam nodded eagerly. "Yes, I'm excited to hear what you have in mind. I really need help with staying on track."

Ms. Lee led them to a quiet corner of the library where they could talk. "Let's start by discussing your current challenges. What's been working, and what hasn't?"

Sam took a deep breath. "I've been trying to follow a routine, but I keep forgetting to stick to it. I've got a garden to take care of, running goals, and a book I want to finish, but I keep losing track."

Ms. Lee listened attentively. "I understand. It's common to struggle with goal-setting and remembering tasks with ADHD. Let's talk about three tools that can help you manage your goals better," Ms. Lee began. "These will make it easier for you to remember what you need to do and help you feel less overwhelmed."

1. Build a Routine:

"Building a routine means doing things in the same order, at the same time, every day," Ms. Lee explained. "Why is this important? Because when you do something regularly, your brain starts to remember it automatically, like brushing your teeth. It makes it easier to remember your tasks without needing to think about them too much. For example, if you always water your garden right after breakfast, it becomes a habit, and you won't forget it as easily."

2. Use Reminders:

"Reminders are like little helpers," Ms. Lee continued. "When you have ADHD, it can be easy to forget things. Reminders, like sticky notes, alarms, or even apps, help keep you on track. Why do you need them? Because they prompt you to remember what you need to do, exactly when you need to do it. Set an alarm for your reading time or use sticky notes on the fridge to remind you to water your plants. These cues help your brain focus and remember better."

3. Try Time Blocking:

"Time blocking means setting aside specific amounts of time for each activity," Ms. Lee said. "Why is this useful? Because it helps you know exactly how much time to spend on each task, so you don't feel overwhelmed or unsure about what to do next. For example, you might set 10 minutes for watering the garden, 15 minutes for running, and 20 minutes for reading. This way, you know exactly what you're doing and for how long, which makes it easier to stay focused."

Sam nodded, feeling a spark of motivation. "These sound like great tools, Ms. Lee! I'm excited to try them out."

Ms. Lee handed Sam a colorful planner with stickers and sections for different tasks. "This planner will help you keep track of your goals.

"Remember, Sam," Ms. Lee added, "it's okay to make mistakes and ask for help. These tools are here to make things easier, and you'll find the ones that work best for you as you keep trying."

Sam took the planner with a sense of excitement. "I'll start using this right away.

As they left the library, Sam felt a renewed sense of hope. With Jake's encouragement and Ms. Lee's guidance, he felt more confident about managing his goals. The journey ahead was still challenging, but he knew he wasn't alone.

Sam and Jake decided to spend some time at the park, where they talked about their plans and supported each other. With every step, Sam felt more determined to face his challenges head-on, knowing that with the right support and strategies, he could turn his dreams into reality.

The sun was bright as Sam woke up the next day, ready

to put his new strategies into action. His room was filled with the cheerful colors of his new planner, which he had carefully hung on his bedroom wall the previous night. The colorful stickers and checklists were a reminder of his goals, and Sam was determined to stick with them.

He started by reviewing his plan for the day: watering the garden, going for a run, and reading a chapter of his book. Sam felt a sense of optimism as he prepared for the tasks ahead.

In the kitchen, his mom was making breakfast. "Good morning, Sam! How's the new planner working out for you?"

Sam grabbed a piece of toast and smiled. "Good morning, Mom. I'm excited to use it today. I've got a list of things to do, and I'm going to try my best to stick to it."

His mom nodded encouragingly. "That's great to hear. Remember, it's okay if things don't go perfectly. What's important is that you're giving it your best effort."

Over the next few days, Sam put Ms. Lee's advice into practice. He started building a routine, setting reminders, and using time blocking to manage his tasks. Here's how each tool helped him:

Sam chose specific times each day for his activities. He watered his garden right after breakfast, went for his run before dinner, and read a book before bed. Slowly, these activities became part of his daily routine

He noticed that by following the routine, he felt more organized and less likely to forget what he needed to do.

Sam put sticky notes in prominent places around his house. A note on the fridge reminded him to check the garden, an alarm on his phone reminded him to start his run, and another sticky note on his bookshelf encouraged him to pick up his book.

These reminders helped Sam stay on track and made it easier for him to remember his goals.

Sam used a simple timer to allocate specific periods for each task. He set 10 minutes for watering the garden, 15 minutes for running, and 20 minutes for reading. By sticking to these time blocks, he felt less overwhelmed and more focused on completing each task efficiently.

After breakfast, Sam headed to the garden, armed with his new planner. He had planned to water the garden and check on the plants. As he began watering, he noticed that some of the plants were still struggling. He felt a pang of frustration.

"Why isn't this working?" Sam muttered to himself. "I'm trying so hard, but it feels like nothing's changing."

Just then, Jake appeared at the garden gate, ready for their morning run. "Hey, Sam! How's the garden coming along?"

Sam looked up, his face showing his concern. "It's been tough. I'm trying to follow the plan, but I feel like I'm not making much progress. Some of the plants still look sick."

Jake stepped into the garden and examined the plants. "It takes time for plants to recover. Have you checked the soil or added any nutrients?"

Sam shook his head. "I haven't done that yet. I've just been focusing on watering them."

Jake nodded. "Maybe we can look into some gardening tips together. It might help to add some fertilizer or adjust the watering schedule."

Sam agreed, feeling grateful for Jake's support. "Thanks, Jake. I'll look into that. It's good to have someone to help me figure things out."

The two friends headed out for their run, and Sam tried to push his worries about the garden to the back of his mind. As they ran, Jake talked about ways to make running more enjoyable, like setting mini-goals and tracking progress.

"You know," Jake said, "sometimes it helps to set small, achievable goals for each run. Like running a little farther each day or timing yourself and trying to beat it. It makes it more fun and gives you a sense of accomplishment."

Sam nodded. "That sounds like a good idea. I'll try to set some mini-goals for my runs."

When they finished their run, Sam was sweaty but energized. He felt a sense of accomplishment, even if it was just a small step. He thanked Jake for the motivation and headed home to work on his reading.

Later that afternoon, Sam sat down with his book. He had set a timer on his phone to remind him when it was time to read. He was excited to dive into the story but found it hard to focus. His mind kept drifting, and he struggled to stay engaged.

Frustrated, Sam closed the book and checked his planner. He saw the sticker that said "Read" and felt a twinge of disappointment. "Why is this so hard?" he asked himself.

His mom walked in and noticed his frustration. "How's the reading going, Sam?"

Sam sighed. "I'm having trouble focusing. I set a timer and everything, but I keep losing my place and getting distracted."

His mom sat down beside him. "It's okay to have those moments. Maybe you can try breaking the reading into smaller sections or finding a quiet spot where you can concentrate better."

Sam nodded. "I'll try that. It's just hard to stay focused."

His mom gave him a reassuring smile. "You're doing great, Sam. It's all about finding what works best for you and sticking with it. Remember, progress takes time."

Feeling a bit more encouraged, Sam decided to break his reading into shorter sessions. He chose a cozy spot in his room, set a new timer, and tried again. Slowly, he began to immerse himself in the book, making steady progress.

That evening, Sam reviewed his day. He had made some progress in the garden, completed his run with a sense of accomplishment, and managed to read a bit of his book. It wasn't perfect, but it was a step forward.

As he prepared for bed, Sam looked at his planner and saw the checkmarks he had made. Each checkmark felt like a small victory. He was learning to manage his goals, even if it wasn't always easy.

With a deep breath, Sam reflected on the day. "It's been a tough day, but I'm starting to see how the little steps matter. I just need to keep trying and adjust when things don't go as planned."

Sam went to bed feeling hopeful, knowing that with each day, he was getting closer to finding the balance he needed to manage his goals. Tomorrow was a new day, and he was ready to face it with the same determination and support from his friends and family.

The sun rose early, casting a gentle light over Sam's garden. He woke up with a sense of determination, ready to face the day and apply the new strategies he had learned.

Sam had been working hard to follow his routines, but he was starting to feel the weight of the challenges more acutely.

After breakfast, Sam went to the garden, where the plants still looked uneven. The sight of them brought a mix of frustration and resolve. He wanted to make sure his garden thrived, and he knew he needed to stick to his plan.

As Sam worked on the garden, he heard the familiar sound of his friend Jake's footsteps approaching. Jake, ever the cheerful encourager, noticed Sam's furrowed brow and came over to offer support.

"Hey, Sam," Jake said, his voice full of enthusiasm. "How's the garden looking today?"

Sam wiped his brow and sighed. "It's still not great. Some of the plants don't seem to be growing, and I'm worried I'm doing something wrong. I've been following the plan, but it feels like it's not enough."

Jake took a look at the garden and nodded thoughtfully. "Gardening can be tricky, especially when you're just starting out. Maybe it's time to adjust the plan a bit. Have you considered asking for advice from someone with more experience?"

Sam shook his head. "I didn't think about that. I guess I

was trying to do it all on my own."

Jake smiled encouragingly. "It's okay to ask for help. Sometimes, getting a fresh perspective can make all the difference."

Sam thought about Jake's advice and decided to visit a local community garden where experienced gardeners shared their knowledge. He felt a mix of nervousness and hope as he made his way to the garden center.

When he arrived, he was greeted by Mr. Thompson, an older gentleman known for his green thumb. "Good morning! What brings you here today?" Mr. Thompson asked with a warm smile.

Sam took a deep breath. "Hi, Mr. Thompson. I've been having trouble with my garden at home. Some of the plants aren't growing as well as I hoped, and I could really use some advice."

Mr. Thompson nodded understandingly. "I'd be happy to help. Let's take a look at what you've got and see what might be the problem."

As they walked through the garden, Sam explained the issues he was facing. Mr. Thompson examined the plants and offered practical advice on soil conditions, watering techniques, and plant care.

"It sounds like your plants might need more nutrients and a different watering schedule," Mr. Thompson explained. "Sometimes, it's about finding the right balance and being patient."

Sam felt a wave of relief. "Thank you so much for your help. I'll try these new tips and see how things go."

Mr. Thompson gave him a reassuring nod. "Remember, gardening is a learning process. Don't be discouraged by setbacks. Every gardener faces challenges. What matters is how you adapt and keep trying."

With renewed confidence, Sam returned home and made the adjustments to his garden. He used the new tips he had learned and took extra care with his plants. Although it would take time to see the results, he felt more optimistic about his progress.

Later in the day, Sam met with Ms. Lee for their coaching session. He shared his experiences and the advice he received from Mr. Thompson.

"That's great to hear, Sam," Ms. Lee said with a supportive smile. "It's fantastic that you sought out help and learned new strategies. How are you feeling about your progress?"

Sam shrugged. "I'm feeling better. The garden still needs

time to improve, but I'm learning to adapt. I guess the next step is to keep practicing and not get discouraged."

Ms. Lee nodded. "Exactly. It's important to keep moving forward, even when things don't go as planned. Persistence is key.

One week, Sam faced a few unexpected challenges. He had a family event that interrupted his routine, and he found it hard to get back on track. His reminders were still there, but he felt frustrated because the disruptions made it harder to stick to his new plan.

Sam decided to talk to Ms. Lee about these difficulties. "Ms. Lee, I've been using the routine, reminders, and time blocking, but when something unexpected comes up, I have trouble getting back on track. What should I do?"

Ms. Lee listened carefully and nodded. "It's great that you're using these tools, Sam. It's normal to face challenges, especially when things don't go as planned. Here are a few more tips to help you handle these situations better:"

1. Build in Flexibility:

"Sometimes, things don't go as planned, and that's okay," Ms. Lee explained. "Try building a little flexibility into your routine. For example, if you miss watering the garden in the morning, you can make time for it in the afternoon. The key is to not get discouraged. Adjusting your plan can help you stay on track even when things change."

2. Reflect and Adjust:

"After a disruption, take a moment to reflect on what happened and adjust your plan if needed," Ms. Lee said. "If you missed your run because of a family event, think about how you can fit it in later or on another day. Reflecting on what worked and what didn't will help you find better ways to manage your time."

3. Ask for Support:

"Don't forget, you have people who want to help you," Ms. Lee added. "Talk to your friends, family, or even me if you're struggling. Sometimes, having someone to support and remind you can make a big difference. It's okay to ask for help when you need it."

With these additional tips, Sam felt more confident. He started incorporating flexibility into his routine and learned to adjust his plan when unexpected events occurred.

Ms. Lee encouraged him to keep using his planner and make adjustments as needed. "Remember, it's okay to have setbacks. What matters is how you respond to them. You're doing great by seeking help and staying committed."

As the day came to a close, Sam reflected on the progress he had made. The advice from Mr. Thompson, the support from Jake, and the guidance from Ms. Lee had given him new insights and motivation. He was beginning to understand that setbacks were a natural part of the process and that asking for help was a strength, not a weakness.

As he prepared for bed, Sam felt a sense of accomplishment. He had faced challenges, learned from them, and continued to pursue his goals with determination. He knew that the journey was far from over, but he was ready to face it with newfound confidence and a supportive network by his side.

The morning sun bathed Sam's garden in a warm, golden light. He stepped outside with a renewed sense of purpose, eager to see how the new strategies he had implemented were working. The plants seemed a bit perkier, and Sam felt a flicker of hope. Today was the day he would continue to push forward, tackling his goals with determination and the support he had received.

As Sam bent down to check on his garden, he noticed that some plants were indeed showing signs of improvement. The once droopy leaves were starting to stand tall. He felt a surge of pride and excitement.

Just then, Jake arrived, looking ready for their morning run. "Hey, Sam! How's the garden looking today?"

Sam grinned, showing Jake the progress. "It's looking better! I followed the advice from Mr. Thompson, and I think it's working. The plants are starting to look healthier."

Jake's eyes widened in admiration. "That's awesome! It's great to see your hard work paying off. Ready for our run?"

Sam nodded enthusiastically. "Definitely. I'm feeling really motivated today."

As they ran through the park, Sam and Jake chatted about their goals. Jake noticed Sam's improved attitude and asked, "So, how's the running going? Are you sticking to your mini-goals?"

Sam puffed slightly, trying to keep pace. "Yes! I've been setting small goals for each run, like running a bit farther or trying to beat my previous time. It's been challenging, but I'm seeing some progress."

Jake smiled. "That's fantastic! Mini-goals are a great way to stay motivated. Keep up the good work!"

After their run, Sam and Jake stopped for a quick break on a park bench. Sam took out his planner and showed Jake his progress. "I've been using this planner to track my goals. It's really helping me stay organized and focused."

Jake glanced at the planner, impressed. "That's a great idea. It's helpful to see everything laid out like that. What about your reading goal?"

Sam nodded. "I've been setting aside time each day to read. It's been tough to stay focused, but I'm making progress. I've finished a few chapters and am starting to see how the book fits into my overall goal."

Jake patted Sam on the back. "You're doing an amazing job, Sam. It's great to see you making strides in all your goals."

Feeling energized from the encouragement, Sam returned home and sat down with his book. He had found a quiet spot in his room where he could concentrate better. The progress he had made with the garden and running gave him confidence that he could tackle his reading goal as well.

As he read, he used a highlighter to mark important passages and take notes. Each small achievement felt like a victory, and Sam was learning to appreciate the process.

Later that evening, Sam met with Ms. Lee for their weekly coaching session. He was excited to share his progress.

"Hi, Ms. Lee!" Sam said, taking a seat. "I've made a lot of progress with my goals. The garden is looking better, my running is going well, and I'm keeping up with my reading."

Ms. Lee beamed with pride. "That's wonderful to hear, Sam! It sounds like you've found a good rhythm with your goals. What strategies have worked best for you?"

Sam thought for a moment. "Using my planner has really helped me stay organized. Setting mini-goals for my runs and breaking my reading into smaller chunks has made it easier to manage."

Ms. Lee nodded. "It's great to see you using these strategies effectively. Remember, progress is often made in small steps. Keep celebrating your achievements, no matter how small they may seem."

Sam smiled. "I'm learning that it's important to acknowledge the small wins. It keeps me motivated and helps me stay on track."

As the session came to a close, Sam felt a sense of accomplishment. He had faced challenges, learned from his experiences, and found strategies that worked for him. His journey was far from over, but he felt more confident and hopeful about the future.

As he prepared for bed, Sam reviewed his planner once more, noting the checkmarks and progress he had made. Each mark was a testament to his persistence and hard work. He felt proud of what he had achieved and was excited to continue pursuing his goals.

Lying in bed, Sam reflected on his journey. "I've come a long way, and I'm learning that persistence really pays off. With the right strategies and support, I can achieve my goals, even when things get tough."

Sam closed his eyes with a sense of satisfaction, knowing that each day brought new opportunities to grow and succeed. Tomorrow was a new day, and he was ready to face it with the same determination and optimism.

As the weeks went by, Sam continued to work on his garden, running, and reading. The initial excitement had begun to fade, and the routines he had established were starting to feel like a heavy weight. Sam found himself struggling to keep up with the daily tasks that once brought him so much joy.

One morning, Sam walked into his garden and noticed that some of the plants were drooping again. His heart sank as he realized he had forgotten to water them for the past few days. He had been so focused on his running and reading goals that the garden had slipped his mind.

"Oh no," Sam whispered to himself, kneeling beside a withering tomato plant. "How could I forget again?"

Sam's frustration grew as he looked around the garden, feeling like all his hard work was starting to unravel. He could feel the old familiar doubt creeping in. Maybe he wasn't cut out for this after all.

Later that day, Sam met Jake for their usual run. But this time, Sam wasn't his usual upbeat self. He dragged his feet as they jogged through the park, his mind weighed down by the thought of his struggling garden.

Jake noticed Sam's quiet mood and slowed down to walk beside him. "Hey, Sam, what's up? You seem really down today."

Sam sighed heavily. "I messed up, Jake. I forgot to water the garden, and now some of the plants are dying. I'm just so frustrated with myself. It's like I can't keep up with everything."

Jake stopped and turned to face Sam. "Hey, don't be so hard on yourself. We all make mistakes. You've been doing a great job with everything. Maybe you just need to take a step back and figure out how to manage it all without feeling overwhelmed."

Sam looked down at his running shoes, feeling the sting of disappointment. "I know, but it's like I keep forgetting the important things. I was so focused on my other goals that the garden just slipped my mind. I feel like I'm failing."

Jake put a hand on Sam's shoulder. "You're not failing, Sam. You're learning. You've taken on a lot, and it's okay to struggle sometimes. Maybe we can figure out a way to make it easier for you to remember everything."

Sam nodded, appreciating Jake's support, but he still felt the weight of his own expectations pressing down on him.

After their run, Sam went home and stared at his planner. The pages were filled with notes, reminders, and goals, but it all felt like too much. He picked up the planner and tossed it onto his desk, feeling a sense of defeat.

Just then, his mom walked in and saw the frustration on his face. "Sam, is everything okay?"

Sam shook his head, trying to hold back tears. "I'm just so tired, Mom. I keep forgetting things, and now the garden is suffering because of it. I don't know if I can keep up with all these goals. It's like I'm trying so hard, but it's never enough."

His mom sat down beside him, her expression gentle and understanding. "Sam, I know how much you care about your goals, and I can see how hard you've been working. But it's okay to feel overwhelmed. Maybe we need to take a different approach."

Sam wiped his eyes and looked at his mom. "But what if I keep forgetting? What if I can't do everything I want to do?"

His mom smiled softly. "It's not about doing everything perfectly, Sam. It's about finding what works for you. Maybe we can come up with a new plan together — one that helps you manage your time and energy better."

Sam nodded slowly, feeling a glimmer of hope. "That sounds good. I just don't want to keep feeling like I'm failing."

After Sam expresses his frustrations, his mom takes a deep breath and looks at him with kindness.

"You're not failing, Sam," his mom reassured him. "You're doing your best, and that's what matters. She gently takes his hand and says, "Sam, I've been watching you work so hard on your garden, your running, and your reading. And I know it feels like you're not getting it right, but every time you try, you're learning something new. Repetition is the mother of skill — every time you water your plants, every time you run, every time you pick up a book, you're getting better, even if it doesn't feel like it right now."

Sam listens carefully as his mom continues. "You know, when I was learning to cook, I burned so many meals. It was frustrating, and I felt like giving up. But I kept trying, and each time I made a mistake, I learned something. Eventually, I got better. It's the same with your goals. The more you practice, the more it will become a habit, and the easier it will get. It's okay if you forget sometimes — that's part of learning."

"Sam, it's important to remember that nobody is perfect, and everyone makes mistakes. What matters is that you keep trying and that you're patient with yourself. When you're feeling overwhelmed, it's okay to take a break and ask for help. You don't have to do everything alone."

With his mom's help, Sam starts to see things differently. He understands that it's not about never making mistakes but about learning from them and continuing to practice. They work together to set up his new routines, making them more fun and less stressful. Sam feels a weight lifting off his shoulders as he realizes that he doesn't have to be perfect — he just has to keep trying.

Over the next few days, Sam begins to notice small improvements. He remembers to water his garden more consistently, his plants perk up, and he feels proud of each sticker he adds to the chart. His running becomes more enjoyable as he listens to his new playlist, and he looks forward to his reading time with his mom. Each small win boosts his confidence, reinforcing the idea that repetition and persistence are key.

Sam looks at his thriving garden, feels his stronger legs after a good run, and smiles at the book he's just finished. He thinks back to all the times he felt like giving up, and he realizes that his mom was right — repetition is the mother of skill. Every time he tried again, even after failing, he was building the skills he needed to succeed. Sam understands that his journey isn't about being perfect; it's about continuing to grow and learn, one small step at a time.

He smiles, feeling a surge of pride. He realizes he's come a long way, and his setbacks didn't define him — they were just part of the journey.

Sam feels a renewed sense of confidence. He knows there will still be days when he forgets or feels overwhelmed, but he also knows he has the tools to handle it and the support of those who care about him.

www.ingramcontent.com/pod-product-compliance
Lightning Source LLC
Chambersburg PA
CBHW072130150726

47999CB00005B/2215